I0051868

The Law is an Ass

-make sure it doesn't bite yours!

WHAT A DAY!

律師

Paul Brennan

Author of "Legal Disputes, the Art of War and You"

A **BRIEF BOOKS** *Production*
Law Books that even lawyers can finish

Praise for *Law is an Ass—make sure it doesn't bite yours!*

'A diverse range of topics, such as how to write a will, fight a neighbour, defend intellectual property rights and of course how to deal with lawyers. Legal services can be "cheap, quick excellent" he said "you can have any two of these but not all three. If your lawyer is consistently delivering all three, be suspicious and look for an angle, for example, is he sleeping with your wife.'
Australian Financial Review

'Lawyer Paul Brennan could just have broken new ground for his profession – writing a legal guide with an opening sentence that would make even a judge laugh. "I never realised why people tended to dislike lawyers until I married one – argumentative, prone to making smart comments and costly too." Contains wry humour which manages to take all the considerable wind out of legal gobbledegook while pulling no punches. In short, sharp jabs it demystifies the law and gives legal insights in layman's terms. Paul's book is about helping people avoid the legal labyrinth from which too many people can emerge bloodied and broke after taking the advice of family and friends to "sue the pants off someone.'
Sunshine Coast Daily

'If you have ever signed a contract without reading it properly, or found yourself in an uncomfortable witness box, the outcome could have been less traumatic had you read this book.'
Institute of Chartered Accountants – Charter Magazine

'Lawyers will also find this a useful and amusing reference to have by their side........You'd have to be hard to please not to be laughing continuously.'
NSW Law Society Journal

'It is a useful reference book which gives the reader a laugh as well as knowledge to take through life.'
Buderim Chronicle

'At last someone has put the law into terms that anyone can understand.'
Cam Young, Presenter' ABC Radio

'A law book with cartoons as well as comical comparisons to the Sopranos is definitely worth a read.'
Guy Sweeting, Host/Producer, Southern Cross Ten

'This is a book all Lawyers should read. It will help them to be 'user' friendly. As a client it helped me understand the frustrations of a lawyer dealing with law on my behalf.'
Kuldeep Saran, Businessman, Hong Kong

'The law can enter your life and cause unnecessary stress. This book is an easy way to learn enough about law to avoid those pitfalls and make it work for you.'
Bruce Sullivan, Pace Learning

'Paul Brennan's dry sense of humour is irresistible.'
Peter F.M. Jones, pmlaw, barristers and solicitors, Toronto

'This is a classic book for the small business owner - short, informative, funny and still delivers its message.'
Gordon Cramer, CEO, Radio 4 Small business

'This is a very practical, commonsense guide to using the law to get better control of your personal or business life.'
Michael Perkins, Cropper Parkhill Solicitors, Sydney

'Not bad, but the absence of Latin will disappoint some readers.'
John Fytit, Solicitor

'Educational and entertaining at the same time."
Conor Ward, Lovells, Solicitors

'If you're like me, you avoid lawyers. The law is stiff and lawyers even stiffer. Paul Brennan changes that on both counts. This is a must-have book for all entrepreneurs. It puts you back in charge of otherwise complex issues in a fun (and dare I say 'exciting') way. Go grab it (before you're grabbed!).'
Paul Dunn, Founder ResultsNet, Results Accountants Systems and Results Corporation

'This is law made easy and quick. Perfect for Small Business Owners.'
Annette Sym, Award winning author and Member of the Federal Government Small Business Council

'An interesting legal overview. Good grounding for anyone in sales.'
Jim Nolan, International Sales and Marketing Consultant for well known luxury brands

'Wise Counsel, sage advice, witty. A funny jaunt through the twisted pathways of laws and lawyers. Filled with extremely practical advice, (from when to fire your lawyer to how to ensure that your divorce is cheap) this book should be read by anyone who comes in contact with the law (or, heavens forbid, with lawyers). And that means you!'
Stephen Stern, Corrs Chambers Westgarth Solicitors

'A quick, fun and informative read - perfect for busy directors to get a handle on the law!'
Duncan Schultz, Professional Independent Director, Fellow of the Australian Institute of Company Directors

'A look at the law as you have probably never seen it before. An enjoyable read with some great advice. Worthwhile for Financial Planners and business advisers generally.'
Derek Ambrose, Ambrose Finance

'This book will help any real estate agent grapple with any legal issue.'
Paul Freney, Professionals Real Estate Agents

'Busy Directors need this insight into law internationally and this is an easy way to take it on board.'
Geoff Webster, CEO, FAST Limited

'.....Well that was a very interesting read, an eye opener! Every agent should read this book ...."
Mark Aitkin, Property Mooloolaba

'Excuse me your Honour, but this is a bloody good read with the concise, legal knowledge that accountants, business advisers and their clients need and without the usual "bovine defecation." '
Barry Hely FCPA, Hely CJM Accounting

'Great insight (and a good read) for any investigator or researcher working with lawyers. This book helps to demystify the legal process and explain why lawyers think the way they do."
Craig Douglas, Investigator/Researcher, Nationwide Research Group

'I have enjoyed reading many of Paul's columns dealing with specific topics and am glad to see this book covering a broad range of problems. Paul manages to clearly point out the highlights of complex matters, giving good pointers on how to stay out of trouble (or in some cases, cause trouble). The Law is an Ass is a good guide for individuals and business owners. It is also a surprisingly good guide, and a good read, for lawyers."
Frank A. Archibald, Partner, Barristers and Solicitors, McMillan Binch Mendelsohn, Canada

'I would recommend this book to any estate agent who wants to know more law but was too afraid of being bored to death.'
Donna Turner, Ray White Real Estate

'An interesting insight into relevant aspects of law."
Stephen Porter, Business Development Manager, Commerce Queensland

'Great legal know-how for speakers and any other business advisers."
Lindsey Adams, CEO, Teamocracy

First published in 2006 by Apec Publishing
2nd Edition published in 2016

National Library of AustraliaCataloguing-in-Publication entry:

Author: Brennan, Paul, (1954-)

Title: The law is an ass-make sure it doesn't bite yours!

Edition: 2nd edition.

ISBN: 9780987489432 (paperback)

Subjects: Law - Popular works

Dewey Number: 340

Brief Books, PO Box 27, Mooloolaba, Queensland Australia 4557.
BN22069914 ABN 60 583 357 067. Phone: 617 5438 8199
www.lawanddisorder.com.au

For other publications by the author see http://www.amazon.com/Paul-Brennan/e/B001KMQFEC

Cover design by Luke Perkins Graphics.

Graphics by Joselito Mahilum.

Layout and typesetting by Toni Esser.

Printed by Createspace.

To my uncle, Albert St Leger

my grandmother, Annie Brennan

and all my aunts and uncles.

CONTENTS

FOREWORD

When Paul Brennan, a lawyer (and a Pom at that), first approached me with an idea to publish a newspaper column on the subject of 'you and the law', I was more than a little sceptical.

Lawyers - like financial planners, relationship counsellors and chiropractors – always tend to think their prose is purple and their content compelling. In truth, they usually offer little more than boring plugs for their own business.

So it was with some suspicion that I first opened the envelope that Paul had sent me. I was quite stunned. His columns were terrific. Short, to the point, irreverent, funny.

Here was a lawyer who obviously knew what he was talking about and who could relate really well to readers. As an added bonus, Paul offered a cartoon to illustrate each week's column.

We began running Paul's column each Saturday in the Sunshine Coast Daily (I was editor of the Daily at the time) and it, and he, quickly built up a following.

It's a natural extension for Paul to collate these little legal gems into a book and I'm delighted that his unique brand of humour, coupled with his knowledge of the law, will now find its way to a wider audience.

Peter Owen,
Group Executive Editor APN Newspapers (Australia)

INTRODUCTION

In Dickens' *Oliver Twist*, Mr Bumble was accused of being responsible for his wife's stealing because 'the law supposes that your wife acts under your direction'. He replied, 'If the law supposes that, the law is an ass—an idiot'.

But the law can decide that you are responsible for your wife or your employee's actions. Being aware of the basic principles of the law puts you on the front foot and allows you to take action to avoid most of the usual problems.

This book has emerged from my experience practising law in Europe, North America, Asia and Australia. I have worked as a lawyer for New Scotland Yard, for a large US Multinational, been a partner in two law firms and I now own my own law firm. I have conducted disciplinary proceedings against lawyers and been a tenant barrister in the Middle Temple, London. My travels have shown me that the law everywhere is very similar. Correct handling of the law and lawyers does not differ from country to country and many legal mistakes are universal.

My intention is to give you basic information about the law without burdening you with too much detail. The subjects I have included will give you a strategic overview of how the law works, internationally, so if you are in business in Australia dealing with international clients, or you are an employee of a multinational company and you travel to many places, this book will help. I've tended to concentrate on those legal issues that most often trip people up, the ones that can so easily go wrong.

While I have used some legal terminology, I've kept the language simple. I have ignored the many ifs, buts and exceptions that are the lifeblood of the law. May all lawyers and experts in the fields covered in this book excuse me for my many generalisations.

The book is intended for corporate warriors, small business owners and everyone in between. Real estate agents, financial advisers, accountants and other professionals who need a legal overview will also benefit from reading this book. My hope is that you will gain a painless understanding of the law—and be amused along the way.

I have divided the law, and the book, into five areas-

* Individual Law including arrest, divorce, lawyer management, neighbour disputes.

* Business Law including buying a business, shareholders' agreements, loans and contracts.

* Suing and being sued including defamation, injunctions, mediation and being a good witness.

* Intellectual property including copyright, trade marks and confidentiality.

* e-law including internet law, emails and spam.

Because the law is not an exact science, remember, legal matters can often turn on the interpretation of one sub paragraph and therefore, on occasions, you will need to seek legal advice from a lawyer.

So, if your wife, like Mr Bumble's, is a little light fingered, the law now says she is not only on her own, but you can have the satisfaction of giving evidence against her. Now that is what we lawyers call progress.

Paul.Brennan@brennanlaw.com.au

The Law is an Ass – make sure it doesn't bite yours!

PART 1

Individual Law

Some situations with legal implications can be a threat to anyone, no matter who you are. Whether you are the Chief Justice or merely a small business owner, these events can have a marked effect on your life and your family.

Many are simply avoided. For instance-

- if you make a will then you can avoid your family brawling after your death

- the best way to lose the tranquillity of your home is to fight with your neighbours

- your world will be turned upside down by a divorce.

If this is so obvious, if you know all this then why do so many people consult lawyers on these issues? Because lawyers can help you avoid the more obvious pitfalls.

1. Managing your lawyer—be firm

I never realised why people tended to dislike lawyers until I married one—argumentative, prone to making smart comments and costly too. If you are tired of changing lawyers or you live with one twenty-four hours a day, like me, the solution is to build a relationship.

I hear you say, 'Shouldn't the lawyer be doing this as part of the service?'

Hey, these are lawyers we are dealing with here!

Don't just moan and put up with it. That will affect your business. Your choice is to either sack 'em or lower your expectations. After years of moaning about lawyers the best way of lowering your expectations is to accept that, all along, you have been the problem. (I did not say this was going to be easy.)

Now here are five questions that may help you examine your conscience in this matter-

1. Are your matters always urgent? Does the material become non-urgent once the ball is in your court?

2. Is the quality and service from your lawyer never really up to scratch?

3. Do you invariably complain about the bill?

4. Do you then call the lawyer and try to get him/her to repeat steps 1 and 2 followed by your steps 3 and 4?

5. Do you then, in exasperation, look for a new lawyer?

Does any of this sound familiar?

Legal services can be cheap, quick, excellent. You can have any two of these but not all three. Cheap and excellent but not quick. Excellent and quick but not cheap. You get the idea. If your lawyer is consistently delivering all three, be suspicious and look for an angle, for example, is he sleeping with your wife?

I hope this helps. Otherwise, keep on sacking—you never know, one day your prince will come.

LAW SCHOOL DAY 1

2. Being arrested—what you need to know

Joe Orton said, 'Reading isn't an occupation we encourage among police officers. We try to keep the paperwork down to a minimum.'

Not only do the police have to deal with the dregs of society but also smug, patronising comments from the likes of Orton. You and I, as right thinking people, believe that the police have a difficult job and for the most part, they carry it out cheerfully and patiently. That is, of course, until you or more likely your son, gets into trouble with the police. Within minutes, you start to go over to Joe Orton's way of thinking.

The Law is an Ass – make sure it doesn't bite yours!

The police, to their credit, by and large, do seem to put guilty people before the courts. Mostly these people plead guilty. Therefore, if you or your son is arrested then, as far as the police are concerned, you are guilty. Worse still, you probably will be guilty.

Let's say, for argument's sake that you are arrested by the police for no reason at all (not an uncommon defence). You are entitled to a lawyer. Will you offend the policeman by calling a lawyer? Has he or she the professionalism to respect your legal rights? The answer is, 'Who cares?' Call the lawyer.

If you feel you can convince the police that they are making a big mistake and there is nothing suspicious about your conduct (bearing in mind you have been arrested and are in a police cell) then make a full statement to the police. If not, your lawyer will advise you to stay stumm and tell it to the court.

By saying things to the police you helpfully add to their evidence against you. Why do you think they go to lengths that would impress even Joe Orton to write down what you say or tape record it?

So, if you are in trouble with the police, get a lawyer and **STAY STUMM**.

I'VE SENT THE KIDS TO BED AND THAT IS THAT

YES, BUT FOR SIX MONTHS!

律師

MAGISTRATES AT HOME

3. Your money lives on when you are gone

Anyone who has watched Midsummer Murders on TV will know how unexpectedly death can occur.

As distressing as your death might be, handled properly it is a fantastic tax avoidance event. With a well set-up trust, your business affairs can continue and no one need miss you at all (so accountants say). However, leave a mess and your relatives must sort it out, as well as coping with their abject grief at losing you.

There are three steps to putting your legal affairs in order prior to your immediate demise.

STEP 1 A WILL

Many of you might prefer to leave this detail until you are on your deathbed. Apart from causing your lawyer to run around like a scalded cat it can be a prelude to the family dividing between those who were at the deathbed and who, coincidentally, benefited from the will, and those who couldn't make it and lost out.

STEP 2 AN ENDURING POWER OF ATTORNEY

This enables one, two or more people chosen by you (called attorneys) to deal with your affairs if you are in a coma or otherwise lost your marbles. You must trust your attorneys absolutely. In the past, this power has been used by unscrupulous individuals (children) to disadvantage other individuals (the other children). So choose carefully.

STEP 3   AN ADVANCE HEALTH DIRECTIVE

This is called various names in different countries but gives much detail on how you wish to be treated (medically) if you are unable to say yourself. It can be, in effect, a Do Not Revive notice. It tells your relatives when to turn the machine off and, in some cases, when to keep their fingers off the button. Without it, typically, there can be fights between your parents, friends, relatives who want to keep the machine on and your spouse who has moved on and wants closure. An advance health directive can avoid all this.

Look on the bright side—you may die, but your money and property live on.

4.   Secret to a comfortable old age—score in another's will

We all know we should make a will, but if you don't you may be long gone before it becomes a problem to those you leave behind. However, from your point of view it is absolutely unacceptable for anybody who may leave his or her money to you to die without one.

Now this has some implications. It is no longer enough to look after your immediate family and the occasional rich uncle. With the property boom even your most despised ne'er do well relatives could leave substantial sums to you, providing you are prepared to put yourself out a bit and, of course, put aside the bitterness of the years.

For those who can forbear from fighting with relatives and neighbours there is a killing to be made. Ironically, the more disagreeable the relative, the nearer you are to the top of the list as they may have fallen out with every other potential beneficiary.

But what if your relatives, friends and acquaintances are as useless and tight as you are as far as wills are concerned? Well, the most reliable but regrettably, illegal method, is to forge their will yourself. Alternatively, in emergencies, aggression and insistence can be presented as being thoughtful and well meaning. However, the safest approach by far is persuasion.

There are many persuasive reasons for making a will. For instance, there is nothing more satisfying than writing someone out of your will. However, you need to make one first. Once you have a will then writing someone out can be done cost effectively by codicil. Or you can decide on a complete redraft of the will to shake up all your beneficiaries.

THE READING OF THE WILL

The secret of a happy and comfortable old age is to ensure that your relatives, neighbours and friends make wills. So get on with it.

5. Where there's a will, there's a way...to ensure your wishes are fulfilled

Do you have a few bob? If so, read on. If not, then this is not for you.

With wills, as in some other situations in life, size matters. Compare the size of your will with those of your friends. Some will have a whooping nineteen pages, which, you may feel, puts your small three-pager to shame.

'But why bother?' as a client asked me the other day. He has one wife and one child. He plans to leave his wealth to her, and if she dies before he does, then he will leave it to his son. His son is capable, not a spendthrift, does not have a drug problem, is happy, hard working, mentally and physically sound. At that stage of the interview I began to doubt that it was his son, but that is by the by.

A standard will seemed to fit his situation exactly. But things change. He could die for instance. With such an attractive wife, no doubt someone else would snap her up. Could this new man set about spending the money? Could his wife die and leave it to the new man so his inheritance does not reach his son? Can the tax

律師
BRENNAN

THERE WAS NO ESCAPING THE
FINANCIAL PLANNER THIS TIME

department be trusted? Could they decide to change the rules to take a cut of his money on death?

A long will is packed with options for your executors. It can still do everything that a standard will can do, if that is the best thing for your beneficiaries. However, if you need a testamentary trust or some other clever device to protect your money then it gives your executors that option too.

One size does not fit all in the wills game. Be warned.

6. Left out of a will? Make a claim

Been left out of a will lately?

Basically, there are three arguments to put to contest a will-

*   The will was not properly drawn up. Although courts are becoming a little less formal, they will still throw out wills for this reason.

*   The deceased was out of his or her mind. If you are an ageing parent get your doctor to witness your will. A doctor's opinion that you are sane is good evidence and may surprise your spouse at the time of making the will.

*   You are a spouse, child or dependant without proper maintenance and support. This is the least dramatic option. Dependant includes anyone the deceased was maintaining or supporting. But not an accountant, no matter how traumatic the death of their client may be.

The court can give you what they think fit, taking into account your financial position, how much money the deceased left and who else is claiming. The older the child, the less likely the court will award something. A child over, say fifty, can claim a 'buffer against misfortune'. The old buffer argument.

You don't need to be on the poverty line but the court recognises that your parents or spouse should still carry you a bit. The courts support people with impairments that prevent them from earning. To come under this category, bone idleness and an inability to get on with employers, ideally, should be described using medical jargon.

For ex-spouses the court will take into account the effort that you put in to building the deceased's estate as well as your conduct, which is often helpfully outlined in the affidavits of the other relatives.

The good news for the challengers is that the legal costs of contesting a will, which can be substantial, are usually paid for from the deceased estate. This is, of course, the bad news if you should win.

律師

THE MAKING TEDIOUS
IRRITATING POINTS TEST
LAW SCHOOL FINALS

7. Divorce—the great frontier

The New Year marks the start of the divorce lawyer's busy season. Married couples around the world are emerging from the trenches of what is paradoxically called The Season of Good Will to launch themselves with gusto into the divorce courts.

Paul Simon suggested that there are fifty ways to leave your lover. In a divorce situation, they all seem to involve the slamming of doors and shouting. Even though most of us will decide to give it another year, it may be an opportune time to consider the Three Rules of Divorce—the Three D's.

DIVORCE RULE 1

Do nothing to wind your partner up. Now if you really cannot resist fighting with your spouse maybe you are not ready for divorce. In divorce, the more satisfying the insult the more it will cost you in legal fees to sort it out. So in divorce be nice to your spouse. Where children are involved this will help keep a semblance of goodwill, which you will need in the ensuing years.

DIVORCE RULE 2

Don't make any quick decisions. Try not to be motivated by feelings of bitterness and anger. Whether you finally decide on counselling or a ruthlessly executed departure (a little like The Godfather when the family moved to Las Vegas), a bit of thought can help you do it better. List the assets you should identify and secure anything that is not nailed down, such as bank accounts. (I am assuming that you may not be the only one in your marriage who is thinking about divorce.)

DIVORCE RULE 3

Do speak to your lawyer before doing anything. At a time when you are too emotionally involved to make rational decisions lawyers are a disinterested party—in some cases a little too disinterested you may feel, so choose carefully. Lawyers can give you the sensible, objective advice that you need.

There is one question that every intending divorcee asks—'Is divorce expensive?' Answer: 'It doesn't need to be'.

8. Winning the backyard battle

When you have the house, wife, two kids and the car and you are living the modern middle-class dream, what new frontiers can the red-blooded male conquer? Those that abut his own garden.

As people live closer and closer together, neighbour disputes are increasingly common. Dogs, children, fences, wives, noise—there is plenty to disagree about. I won't go into tactics but you may find *The Art of War* by Sun Tse Tzu to be particularly useful.

Like some magistrates, the police can be swayed by a well-presented case. That's why it is best to avoid disputes with criminals, as they don't fear arrest and they have a good working knowledge of the laws of evidence gained through grim experience.

How do you put together a well-presented case? Well, one person's word against another is not good enough. What you need are independent witnesses (no relatives). Expect your complaint to be met with a counter complaint. Therefore, while building your case you must insist on iron discipline within your own family.

What type of evidence do you need? Well, shouting is okay to show intent especially if there are threats of violence. But what you are really looking for is some violence towards you, or preferably, your wife. Most families have video cameras. Use them.

Provocation is no defence against a criminal charge unless, of course, you kill your neighbour. In the case of murder, you will need full details of your neighbour's irritating conduct to gain valuable years off your sentence.

If keeping on good terms with your neighbour is increasingly difficult and you want to avoid the hassle, the best option is to move. So will your neighbour's criminal trial and conviction be the end of the matter? Of course not, but some would view it as a very satisfying start.

The answer is to take your frustrations out on waiters, bank clerks, taxi drivers, motorists and others of modest stature who don't know where you live and leave your neighbour alone.

9. Delegating control is a matter of trust

Trusts are all the rage.

To create a trust is easy. It starts with a thirty-plus page trust deed, which allows you to hand all, or some of your money, to a completely separate entity so you do not control it anymore. Why would anyone want to do that? Well people get worried about being sued and losing the lot; or their ex-spouse finding it; or their accountant says it's a good way to save tax; or it's cheaper to set up than a company.

There are three major players in the trust world.

The Trustee is generally a long-suffering individual who is chosen to be the gatekeeper of someone else's fortune. They harbour thoughts of throwing off their responsible image and doing a runner to Rio—few make it. Trustees are often suspected of torturing difficult beneficiaries by giving them their inheritance on a drip, drip basis.

THE CLIENT COULDN'T PAY

律師

LAWYER HORROR MOVIES

The Beneficiary can slouch around, waiting to be paid, grouching and whingeing about how the trustee is not doing a good job. Yes, it is a lot of fun. Beneficiaries of discretionary trusts are a little better behaved as the trustee decides who gets the money and in some trusts, the trustee can decide not to give anyone anything. This leads to the phenomena of 'trustee's pet' for those beneficiaries who know which side their bread is buttered.

The Appointor is a shadowy figure who works behind the scenes and usually decides how the trustees are dismissed and who replaces them. If he does not like what the trustees are doing, he sacks them. Making yourself the appointor allows you to call the shots and continue to control your fortune.

Trusts have drama, intrigue and can be a great source of entertainment in your declining years.

10. The man with four lawyers

The other day I met a man with four lawyers from separate law firms. In biblical times they had plagues of various things but not even Job was afflicted by four lawyers. Lawyers are serious professionals, not collector's items. I don't think even Imelda Marcos had four lawyers.

People nowadays increasingly want specialists. The problem is that without a form book and some inside knowledge you will find it difficult to pick a winner. Also, the solution suggested by the specialist you choose must not only be proportionate to your problem but also to your ability to pay. Your own general practice lawyer will be in a good position to assess this.

The Law is an Ass – make sure it doesn't bite yours!

So here are three minimal standards you should look for in a lawyer-

1. Must be a human being. Strangely this is not a Law Society or Bar requirement. How will you know if your lawyer is from the Planet Zog? Well movies like Alien and ET may help. But we do have some lawyers who were formerly accountants and therefore, being dull and a little strange is not a sufficient indication.

2. Must be available. Is your lawyer like the Scarlet Pimpernel? Do you find yourself seeking him here and seeking him there without much success?

3. Must be able to operate the telephone. Some lawyers have had difficulty adapting to this new technology. But please remember that lawyers usually charge on a time basis, so every time your lawyer returns your call it costs you money. Therefore if your lawyer doesn't say much but delivers (not unlike Clint Eastwood) it is cheaper to let him get on with it.

If you are not that happy with your lawyer, then change. Although it may be more satisfying to stay and make your lawyer's life a misery it is not good for your own business. Find someone who suits you.

Maybe you need a specialist and maybe you don't. Why not speak to your own general practice lawyer first who will tell you if you need a specialist and make a recommendation. Don't follow advertisements or marketing claims.

But as vital as legal advice sometimes may be, I still think four lawyers is not the answer. If God wanted us to have multiple lawyers he would have given us all more money for a start.

PART 2

Business is Business

If you are in business you need a good lawyer. A good lawyer is someone you trust and someone who keeps you out of trouble. It's a partnership and a lawyer you trust can help you get the right balance between seeking legal advice too often, which can be unnecessarily costly in legal fees, and not seeking enough advice, which can leave you exposed to other problems and potentially higher costs.

Some legal issues arise repeatedly in business. Being forewarned is being forearmed.

1.   Heed the bank's advice

Banks say they love you and trust you but when you get there you find they've chained the pens to the counter. A client whose business had been sent to the wall commented the other day that being with the same bank for thirty years seemed to count for nothing.

It is true that banks are ready to put aside a relationship of many years to get their money back. This does not make your bank the Great Satan although, as your finances worsen, it may seem that way.

Let's get expectations straight. What can banks do? They can enforce the loan against you and anyone else who has guaranteed your debt. So, for example, if you or your guarantor has a house, the bank can force you to meet the market. This might mean selling your property at auction for whatever price you can get, however low. Depressing stuff.

In this scenario, the bank manager is not a Dr Evil or Mini Me (although the likeness can be uncanny). In fact, the bank manager is a very good source of information and wise counsel. They have seen it all before. To alienate your bank manager would be a mistake.

If your business is going bad, at some stage your bank manager will stop lending to you. This is not a cue to borrow money from your family in order to make loan repayments to the bank. Parents, it is not a cue to bail out your child, again! Nor is it the signal to put your bank loan repayments on your credit card. Your bank manager's refusal to continue lending to you is an excellent assessment of your position. Heed it.

So what can lawyers do? Fight the rap! A lawyer can establish that when you guaranteed the debts of your son you did not know that it meant you would have to pay for his mistakes (as if you haven't been paying for his mistakes your whole life). This tactic has been used successfully, however, in my experience, this is not the time to spend money on legal fees. It's the time to throw yourself into the arms of your accountant. And that is why you should pick a good-looking one while there is still time.

2. Should tenants hate those leases to pieces?

Landlords are not nice people. Something seems to come over people who own property and rent it out. Once you understand that they get a lot easier to deal with.

I know some people who may not be landlords but who instinctively have the temperament for it. On the other hand, most landlords struggle to be nasty—but we all usually manage it in the end.

The main tool of the landlord is the lease. When landlords select a form of lease they generally opt for the Terminator variety rather than the Winnie the Pooh model. Leases are a minefield for the unwary. They contain delayed action mines that can go off months or years later—usually when your business is facing its darkest hour. With most new businesses failing within the first two years you can probably understand why landlords are a little paranoid.

Even after trying to find out where to sign, sometimes made easier by helpful red *sign here* stickers, often commercial leases remain unread by the tenant, all twenty-five plus pages!

律師

COURT ROOM HUMOUR

Here are just a few things that can go wrong-

• No assignment clause. This means you cannot offload the lease if you run into trouble.

• You assign the lease to another but you remain liable for their non-payment, or non-payment by anybody they assign it to. Options to renew are better than one long lease period.

• If you secured a bargain rent, or at least one that you could afford, then watch out for a market review after one year which could make the rent go way up.

I know I can't deter the red-blooded prospective tenant from the 'Just do it' approach. It certainly worked for Nike.

But leases are what lawyers do well. Some lawyers even enjoy reading leases. Sad, but useful if you are a tenant who doesn't want to lose his shirt.

3.   Contracts that numb the brain

In Queensland, Australia, where I now practise law, the estate agents have produced a standard conveyancing contract. It would be churlish of me to point out that this is the lunatics taking over the asylum however, one slight criticism of the Queensland Real Estate Institute's Standard Contract for Commercial Land and Buildings (4th ed.) is that it bores the pants off people.

Where is that estate agent pizzazz? Shouldn't there be exciting references like water rate glimpses; just a few minutes from the breach; or, warranties that must be seen to be believed? In fact, it is so boring it looks like lawyers put it together and have somehow convinced the real estate agents to carry the can.

Most people can't be bothered to read legal documents. Who can blame them? Well, judges can. For hundreds of years, courts have listened to people saying they did not know what they were signing. Generally, if you sign a contract then you are stuck with it. Consumers get some leeway, but not business owners.

In the old days it was like 'Where's Wally' to find the detail in a contract. Now all the excitement has been taken out of it because the important details are mostly thrown in a schedule where anyone can find them.

As a buyer what should you be concerned about?

- Keep an eye on the deposit you pay. What happens to it? Is it invested? Where?

- If the building burns down after you sign the contract are you responsible? Usually, yes. So you may need to insure immediately the contract is signed.

- Anything not nailed down can be removed if not specifically mentioned. Gain access to the premises before completion to check the inventory and state of repair.

ANOTHER SUCCESSFUL CONVEYANCE

律師

CONVEYANCING LAWYER DREAMS

- The contract should be subject to your obtaining finance and satisfactory pest and building inspection reports. So if you can't get a loan to buy the house or the house turns out to be a wreck you can get your deposit back and walk away.

- At settlement, ask for all the documents, not just the keys.

All this and more is covered by the Queensland real estate agent's contract in mind-numbing detail and lawyers just love it. But we would, wouldn't we?

4. Success can be a major problem

A big problem for small business is success. Say you have gone into business with an equal shareholder (a partner) and managed not to go bust in the first two years.

With success comes a need for structure to maximise the benefit of your successful business idea. A first step is to introduce a written shareholders' agreement.

Without one you are looking for trouble if your partner is undisciplined, dies, goes gaga, becomes bankrupt, decides to leave, wants to set up on their own next door taking the business (without you), or is just too generous with company information. A shareholders' agreement will help in resolving disputes or if you want to bail out.

There is no standard shareholders' agreement but here are five possible benefits of having one-

1. Strict guidelines for transfer of shares. You get to choose who you are in business with.

2. A set procedure for valuation and purchase of shares if your partner should want to leave, is ill or dies, or becomes bankrupt. You can arrange insurance to cover the ill or dead shareholders' share, or the agreement can provide for the shares to be purchased over a one year period to ease the burden.

3. A budget and business plan established at the beginning of each year to set a direction for the company. This is important if your partner is a bit of a free spirit, especially with the chequebook.

4. For mediation of disputes. As much as you may enjoy slapping a writ on your partner, disputes are best resolved by mediation— at first anyway.

5. For restraint of trade and confidentiality of information.

Why don't all businesses have a shareholders' agreement? Because they can be thirty pages long, raise difficult issues, are very dull and worst of all, they cost money. However, if trouble breaks out they can deliver peace of mind.

LONGEST TRIAL FINALLY ENDS

5.   Liability rattles the directors

In good times people pay their debts and credit control takes a back seat. There is a corporate veil between a director's money and the company's funds. This means that creditors can sue the company but not the director. This is good and sensible commercial practice unless you are the person who is owed the money and then it becomes a charter for cheats and scoundrels.

In bad times, experienced creditors get in first, make threats and are quick to take court proceedings.

The Law is an Ass – make sure it doesn't bite yours!

Here are a few sabres for creditors to rattle to worry directors-

- Deliberately incurring debts with no chance of paying them back is fraud. If debtors believe that you might call the cops, they are more likely to pay.

- Insolvent trading. This lifts the veil and directors can be held personally responsible.

- An investigation by the body which regulates companies. This raises the prospect of fines and being barred from acting as a director for not being a fit and proper person to manage a company.

- De facto director. You may not have been appointed legally as a director but you may be treated as a director if you have acted like one in fact.

- Shadow director. This targets the Mr Big who is really calling the shots even if he is not legally a director. Some say this is too wide and could be used to trap your bank manager. But who could take any joy out of such an unfortunate consequence?

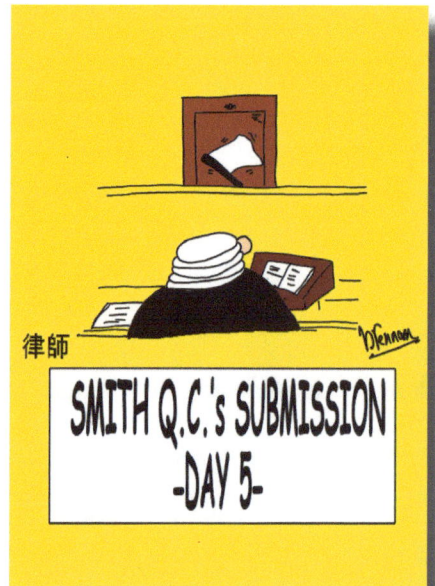

律师

SMITH Q.C.'s SUBMISSION
-DAY 5-

Does all this sound a bit squalid? Well it is. But do it wrong and you could be accused of blackmail.

If being a creditor is a bit tedious then there are always the options of conducting credit checks, insisting on guarantees or taking your customer's mother hostage. However, who has time to plan that sort of thing and run a business?

6.   Beware pests at auction

Property auctions can be fun, but they are very serious business.

Before you go to an auction, have your finance approved in writing and obtain a building and pest report on the property you wish to purchase. This always seems a waste of time but there are pests and some of them are building houses and others are lending money.

As auctions are often held at the property itself you can be sure that you have got the right one. However, your lawyer should look at the title just in case there are problems. What sort of problems? Well legal type problems—they do occur you know.

Before the auction you should decide exactly how high you will bid. This will enable you to panic and raise it just before the auction and then again during the auction.

Auctioneers do not launch into the bidding straightaway. They start with a glowing description of the house. This can be so convincing that some sellers wonder if they are attending the right auction; others change their minds and decide to stay. For the prospective buyer the tension mounts.

The Law is an Ass – make sure it doesn't bite yours!

The bidding starts. At crucial moments when you need to agree a further increase in your bid, comments such as, 'Whose go is it?' at least suggest that your spouse is aware that the auction has started.

You top everyone else's bid. This doesn't satisfy the auctioneer who agonisingly continues to try to squeeze a bid out of anything that moves. Finally, the auctioneer gives up and with a dramatic bang of the hammer, the property is yours. You feel like you have just delivered twins.

GREAT LEGAL MAXIMS...
AS SOBER AS A JUDGE

AS DRUNK AS AN AUCTIONEER

律師

On the fall of the hammer the property goes to the highest bidder. There is no cooling off period, conditional-upon-finance arrangement, building or pest report or much relief from legal problems. You are stuck with it. That is the good news unless there is something wrong with the house and then that is the bad news.

7. Disclaimers—don't blame us

In contracts there is usually a part which says, 'Although we have promised you the earth please don't blame us if anything goes wrong'. This is called a disclaimer.

In some countries like Australia, more often than not, disclaimers are ineffective. The court sees failing to keep your promises as 'misleading and deceptive conduct', and will stop you trying to walk away from your obligations. In other countries, like England, the courts sometimes throw out disclaimers, especially if they seem to have been imposed unfairly, for example, in an unequal bargaining situation. But don't expect to be mollycoddled.

A legal claim can wipe out a small business owner. What are 'weasel words' to a customer are protective armour to the small business owner.

What should small business owners do?

AND I HAVE TAKEN INTO ACCOUNT YOUR PREVIOUS GOOD CHARACTER AND THAT YOU ARE MY MOTHER
BUT . . . . .

*   Include the disclaimer anyway. They do discourage customers making claims or at least make it a little more difficult to claim. The disclaimer may help to convince a customer to be reasonable in any settlement discussions.

- If the customer did not rely on what you said then it was not misleading, however, this is hard to prove. Some owners go to great lengths to explain the obvious, for example, warning— this coffee is hot when poured on the crutch area.

- Impose an upper limit, a cap, on the amount of any claim.

- Impose a limit on the time in which a complaint can be made.

Such limits and caps can work. Certainly look at your competitor's terms and conditions but don't copy them blindly. There is nothing more infuriating than going to the trouble of copying a competitor's terms and conditions only to find that they are useless when trouble strikes.

For many small businesses, the only disclaimer that really works is the one that they sign up to in their own supplier's contracts. So check what you are agreeing to before signing a contract.

8. Why vicarious liability is the weakest link

Say an employee of Woolworths dropped a box of baked bean cans on your foot. You suffer a broken foot. You cannot work and lose wages. You incur medical expenses. Your chances of playing Wimbledon are shattered. You suffer terribly from the pain and cruel 'baked bean' jokes.

Like anyone else in these circumstances you have no hesitation in suing Woolworths. Woolworths argue that they had trained the employee in foot avoidance techniques. Even so, Woolworths is likely to be vicariously liable for its own employee's conduct. If the employee was negligently clumsy then he could be sued as well. However, companies like Woolworths usually pay up and the employee is confined to checkout duties or leaves to become a furniture removalist or accountant.

What if the employee punched every customer who asked a question? Would Woolworths be vicariously liable then? Probably, but the acts must occur in the course of business. This would cover fights whilst on home delivery duties but not violent acts by the employee when travelling to and from work.

Even though you might be a small business owner, you, like Woolworths, are potentially vicariously liable for the deliberate and negligent acts inflicted upon your customers by your employees if done in the course of business. Depending on what your employees are like, this is worrying.

If your employee accuses your competitor of going bust and then, helpfully, circulates the statement by email, you may be liable for his defamatory conduct. In some cases, your documented policies may allow you to avoid liability by demonstrating that the employee had gone off on a frolic of his own.

On the up side, you get the satisfaction of suing your employee for his negligent conduct. But on what you pay, will he ever have enough money to make this worthwhile?

9. Your mortgage—you and a load of old bankers

Ever since the moneylenders were thrown out of the temple, banks have been, and remain unpopular. Message to bank marketing departments: don't worry this is not your fault.

Your lawyer should always review your mortgage documents. Why?

Think of it this way. When a bank compiles its mortgage documents it generally asks itself, 'What would the Sopranos do in this situation?' Banks are not allowed to leave a horse's head in your bed, break your arms or have a 'sleeping with the fishes' clause. However, within these constraints they do their best to draft clauses which make life very difficult

HELL'S BANKERS

律師

BORN TO RAISE INTEREST

for non-payers. For instance, selling your house and making you bankrupt.

Widows, grannies and orphans trying to get out of re-paying bank loans—best of luck. Not even the Godfather was that tough.

Apart from the usual questions about interest rates and the period of the loan, there are probably two things to ask about a mortgage—

1. Can you repay all or some of the money early, without any penalty?

2. What are the bank fees and any other costs of entering into the mortgage?

Neither of these is a legal question and both can be answered at an early stage without your lawyer.

However, a new breed of hero has emerged. These are the local bank managers, many of whom, increasingly, do not seem to like banks either. Their tireless struggles against Head Office are not unlike those by Dr Who against the Daleks—INTEREST RATE, INTEREST RATE, INTEREST RATE.

Although bank managers have lending targets and that means they are increasingly pressured to sell to you, they are usually a great source of frank advice, but you must ask.

Some bankers reading this will be thinking, 'Since when do lawyers have the gall to criticise banks over fees?' Well, at least we didn't get thrown out of the Temple, did we?

10.   Buying a business?

A business owner has a business. It isn't doing so well. Most fail in the first two years so that is nothing new. He approaches investors, but his parents refuse to carry him on this occasion. After all he has done for them!

He considers taking in a partner but there are no takers. He decides to sell. What sort of buyer is he looking for? Prudent? Alert? Or a bit of a mug? You enter at this point and like many buyers, you are excited with the potential and just want to sign up. Even more so when another buyer appears (they always seem to).

Like a house purchase, buying a business is a two-step process. You sign a contract and pay a deposit, then thirty days later you hand over the rest of the money. Easy—but what if the business stinks?

How committed are you in signing a contract? Interestingly, contracts have no legal effect whatsoever. (I am joking—in fact, contracts are legal and intended to commit you as deeply as the seller can get away with.)

The contract is probably subject to finance but apart from that there are other strategies you can use to protect your interests. For instance-

- Work in the business for, say, two weeks and check that it is as profitable as the seller says.

- Have your accountant inspect the books.

If the business does not seem profitable, you get your deposit back and walk away.

As further protection for the buyer, the seller must not set up in competition, and he must pay out existing employees who are not taken on by the new buyer.

In business it is prudent to consult your lawyer and accountant before making crucial commercial decisions. This should be seen as part of the expense of buying a business, however miserable and pedantic both these people may seem at the time.

11.   Restraint of trade

Regrettably, since indentured slavery has been abolished there is no obligation by your employees to continue working under your benign dictatorship until you decide to dismiss them. But what if your most loyal employee leaves you, sets up next door and starts calling your clients? Surely the law will punish such treachery?

Well, it all depends-

- Has the employee stolen your 'crown jewels'? For example, a client list? Let me rephrase that question. Can you prove it?

- Did the employee's contract contain a clause restraining the employee from doing you down? Pulling out the contract and finding a 'restraint of trade clause' is not just good luck—it usually means you have had good legal advice. Important employees handling your best clients should have a contract of employment drawn up by a lawyer.

The restraint clause typically covers three areas-

- the type of business in which your ex-employee cannot engage

- within a certain geographical area

- for a particular length of time.

You need to decide carefully how to adequately protect your business as the court will strike out restraint clauses which they regard as too wide. The court will want to see some evidence of damage to your business.

An employee can take subjective knowledge and know-how. But knowledge in the shape of entire client lists, which he copies or even memorises, he cannot take. Defining the difference between what the ex-employee knows and what he has taken is not easy. A word to those who like to do their own legal work—restraint clauses are not the

律師

LATE AGAIN!
THIS BETTER BE GOOD.

best place to start as they are tricky and striking them out is one of a judge's few pleasures in life.

Most cases turn on their own facts, which can be lawyerspeak for 'we haven't got a clue how this case will turn out, but we are not going to tell you that'.

PART 3

Sue and be Sued

Litigation is legal warfare. Some people approach litigation as if it is a deal where profit may result.

Please understand litigation is not a deal—it is a very stressful pastime. Legal trials are a roller-coaster ride, each day bringing a new high or low as the evidence twists and turns. However, sometimes when all other options have been exhausted there is no choice but to litigate.

1. Litigation—the last resort

It would be great if litigation was like boxing and after a few three-minute rounds one person was declared the winner.

Anyone who has been in litigation will tell you that there is a lot of pleasure in slapping a writ on your enemy. If the credits rolled at that point then it would be a very satisfying experience. But they do not. Litigation is stressful, time consuming and expensive.

Your lawyer will advise you to look for every opportunity to avoid litigation. Both contracts and courts often refer matters to mediation where the parties can reach some common ground to settle their difficulties without a court hearing.

So why litigate? Unfortunately, in business there are people who will treat you as a mug, try to rip you off or just dither. After trying every other avenue even the most prudent business owner is sometimes faced with the prospect of litigation.

Here are four things to bear in mind-

1. However badly your opponent has acted the law only compensates you for your loss. It is not a deal where you might make a profit.

YOU SHALL ALL GO TO PRISON FOR SIX MONTHS

律師

THE JUDGE IS DREAMING

2. If you win, the court will order your opponent to pay your costs. This payment is usually not enough to cover all your legal expenses— only about 70% of them.

3. In litigation the goal posts shift regularly, so make sure of your evidence. Take statements from witnesses to ensure you understand what they are saying and to stop their stories changing. Secure any documents.

4. Most cases settle, often at the court door. So look for settlement and compromise as the matter progresses.

If you are ready to do what it takes and prepare carefully then litigation can be an effective tool to deal with difficult people. It calls their bluff.

2. The limits of what a lawyer will do

If there was an Oscar for the best criminal defence ever it would go to what I know as the 'Jump Up' defence. I don't know why it is called that.

Imagine that you are a criminal. You have just stolen a TV and you are carrying it down the street. A policeman catches you red-handed. Being a criminal you stay stumm (see page 18). At your trial you say that you were walking along the road when a man said to you, 'Do you want to make some cash?' Being out of work, you agreed. The man tells you to pick up a TV and follow him. You were following him, carrying the TV, when the policeman stopped you.

In criminal trials the prosecution must prove the case beyond reasonable doubt so that the jury is sure. Juries often give the defendant the benefit of the doubt especially where the Jump Up defence is used.

So why doesn't everyone plead clever defences like the Jump Up? Well, defence lawyers are not able to assist their clients (even a little bit) in concocting untrue defences. Defendants often learn basic defence strategy in prison, however, it displays a marked lack of creativity. They can't all have brilliant criminal minds. If they were that smart at school they would now be bank managers.

What lawyers will not do is represent you in a not guilty plea to the court if they know you are guilty. I have had to work with some lousy, implausible defences over the years, but some have turned out to be true—so you never know. Therefore, the only way to be sure that your lawyer knows that you are guilty is for you to tell him.

Finally, I suggest that you expect professional detachment from your lawyer rather than tea and sympathy. If you can't do the time, don't do the crime.

THE REAL REASON THAT THE POLICE HANDLE THE EXHIBITS

3. Being a good witness

Have you ever been called to be a witness in court? It is quite nerve wracking.

One witness I cross-examined cried throughout. This made me look like the incisive, hectoring advocate that I had always wanted to be. It also took time. As I was being paid by the day it seemed a rather perfect arrangement to me. However many judges like to rush (as if they had something better to do) and they can get really cross with witnesses who waste time. In fact, they can get cross about almost anything, therefore rule one is, 'Try not to cross swords with the Judge if you can help it'. Tough, I know.

One client of mine, in answer to the question, 'You did this didn't you?' from the opposing lawyer, answered 'Yes'. But who wouldn't break down when faced with such devastating cross-examination?

Such admissions are very rare, or at least I have not seen that happen to any other lawyers.

Just like police interrogations on television there will be two questioning lawyers—one nice and one nasty. The idea is to give short 'yes' or 'no' answers to the nasty lawyer and full explanations to the nice lawyer. Make sure you do this no matter how provocative or plain wrong the nasty questions may seem. Arguing with the nasty lawyer can be fun—but not usually for you.

律師

THE NIGHT BEFORE TRIAL
THE PROSECUTION PUT
THE FINISHING TOUCHES
TO THEIR MAIN WITNESS

There is a Chinese expression about 'putting legs on the snake'. Some witnesses (defence and prosecution) decide to add a few things to their testimony to present a better case. Technically, this is known as lying. Your truthful evidence will stand up by itself. Like the snake, it moves perfectly well. You will not be caught out by cross-examination. It does not need you to add legs.

Of course, for some witnesses telling the truth is not an option.

4. Avoid a verbal beating

A subpoena for the production of documents is a direct command from the Court. If you don't produce the documents you can be arrested, verbally beaten up by a judge and jailed. Contempt of court gets judges so cranky that it takes the heat off the rest of us. Unless you are looking for material for a book or otherwise have a few days or weeks to kill, just comply with the subpoena.

Is it easy for a lawyer to issue a subpoena? Very easy. Although getting the spelling right can be a challenge.

But what if you are asked to produce your trade secrets? Or your therapist or doctor is ordered to hand over notes which reveal your haemorrhoids? Then you have no option but to fight.

Here are four tactics you can use-

1. Is the Subpoena from the Court? A lawyer's letters or telephone calls can be ignored. As well, the documents need only be produced to the Court itself.

2. You must be given:

    a) Your expenses to get the documents to Court

    b) Usually, reasonable notice to produce, for example, fourteen days.

3. You can object to the lawyers that their request is too vague. They may limit their request.

4. If this doesn't work put the documents in a sealed envelope, go to Court and explain to the judge on oath your objection to producing the documents. You can argue that-

    a) they are not relevant

    b) it is unduly burdensome to comply either because of the expense or the request is an abuse of the process.

If it is haemorrhoids then you will find the judge very knowledgeable and sympathetic. If it is something else, like an affair, then the judge may want to go into a little more detail. Regrettably, your privacy or confidentiality is not a reason to refuse to produce documents. But judges can order that the documents be used in a way that saves your face.

THE BASICS

MISERABLE EXPRESSION

SHOT SIGHTED

GLUE EAR

EASILY IRRITATED

NO SENSE OF HUMOR

律師

JUDGES' TRAINING SCHOOL - DAY 1

5. Defamation—easy to do and costly to get over

Defaming someone is easy. Write it down and its libel. Say it and its slander. If you must defame someone then it's best to choose slander because it's harder for someone else to prove what you actually said. However, with the advent of email most people prefer to write their insults down. This is exceptionally good evidence or exceptionally bad evidence depending which side you are on.

It is not enough to insult your enemy to their face—someone else needs to hear to make it defamation. It needs to be 'published'. A letter in a local newspaper is a perfectly adequate way to publish a libel, as is shouting it at the top of your voice. Both are popular methods.

Saying a few bad words about someone is one thing. But the important question is how much damage your words have done, as that will determine the 'damages' (the amount of money to be awarded by a court).

How big is the audience? The circulation of a local newspaper is not bad but you risk the newspaper culling your statement. Newspapers are vigilant, as they too could be liable for defamatory statements appearing in their pages.

Sending a personal email to someone at work, where his boss reads it, is a very small but important audience.

For suggesting that one of your competitors is going out of business you get full marks in the defamation stakes. Most business owners have more sense than to do this, but there are always exceptions. Employers can be vicariously liable for the defamatory statements of their employees, so employers are really at the mercy of their employees.

What if you are the person who has been defamed? First, spend a sleepless night imagining court scenes of cross-examination with you playing a part not unlike Joan of Arc. Next day, visit your lawyer. Defamation proceedings are very expensive and have led, on occasions, to the bankruptcy of one of the parties. Therefore, after the initial upset you may think of other more important ways to spend your money. Your lawyer will advise you to be satisfied with an apology which can be demanded by way of a solicitor's letter.

If you have defamed someone then go to your lawyer who will probably advise you that it is best to apologise and move on. For once, just do what your lawyer says.

6.   What's the damage?

Anyone who has watched US television soap operas will know that a win in a lawsuit is a time for great rejoicing for clients and lawyers alike. This is not the case in the rest of the world. Generally, courts try to return the claimant to the position they were in before they suffered the loss which, for a lot of people, is not so great.

For instance, you are injured in an accident and the insurers have paid you $100,000. Your spouse breaks out the champagne. However, the insurers have carefully calculated your pain and suffering over the next few decades. The more money you get the more you are likely to suffer.

This principle of returning the defendant to their original position applies generally across the board in litigation. Clients want to know if their case is good enough to sue the pants off their opponent. Normally the answer is a resounding 'yes'. However, the real issue is how much the claim is worth, that is, what damages (money) will they receive, if and when they win.

律師

THE MAGISTRATE HAD GONE TOO FAR THIS TIME

For example, where someone has run off with your cash it is easy to determine the damages. You get back the cash. The court does not normally give you a bit extra on top because the defendant has been a real nuisance. The object of an award by a civil court is generally not to punish but to compensate you for your loss. Even with damages which in America would be considered small change, many uninsured defendants go bankrupt. This means claimants go without, however worthy their cause.

But if your main object is to bankrupt your opponent and make them suffer, if financial gain is a secondary consideration—then litigation is for you.

7. Injunctions—stop in the name of the law

In the old days people would rush before the King and demand justice and he would immediately deal with the case. When the King decided to knock that on the head lawyers got hold of litigation and implemented increasingly more longwinded processes.

Today the processes are relatively quick but you still need to jump the hurdles of your lawyer wanting to send a warning letter to the other side, collecting detail and paperwork, taking statements and doing a lot of messing about called solid preparation. It takes weeks before you can slap a writ on your enemy and worse still, they don't even call it a writ anymore.

However, if the matter is urgent, for example, your former employee gives your client list to a competitor or a neighbour threatens to knock down your wall or tree or a nuclear attack is imminent, you can be in court the following morning. In urgent matters a court will order an interim injunction to stop the action until the case can be heard.

But courts do not grant injunctions lightly. There are certain tests that a judge will apply, such as-

1. It's got to be something serious. Anything involving pets, hurt feelings or golf are not going to do it.

2. Is it really necessary? Could a payment (damages) after the hearing be sufficient compensation?

3. The court will try to balance the convenience of granting an injunction to you against the inconvenience to your opponent. For instance, what if you were wrong but the injunction causes your opponent's business to go under?

You must undertake to be responsible for any loss caused by the injunction if you should eventually lose the case.

An application for an interim injunction is quick, exciting and, of course, expensive.

8. Mediate–don't wait

No so long ago there was no real thought of mediation. Clients were advised not to speak to their opponent. A writ would be served and skirmishes could occur right up to the time of the hearing, when a huge number of cases settled at the court door. Few facts were admitted. Communication with what we still call 'the other side' would be, for the most part, aggressive. Early settlement would be initiated by the defendant, if at all. Acting outside these bounds was seen as a sign of weakness. In many instances, this is still the case.

Now, courts frequently refer matters to mediation. Mediation is an opportunity for both sides to consider an early compromise without losing face. There is an expectation that the parties will try to find a compromise, but compromise takes two and therefore, sometimes mediation can be a waste of time.

Mediation is not brain surgery. A mediator is selected by the parties, or the court, and meets with the parties and their lawyers. The mediator is not there to judge but to hammer out a compromise. It can take a day. The parties may start in separate rooms. The mediator flits between rooms seeking common ground. What a party definitely will not agree to at 9 am may seem not such a bad idea at 5 pm in order to get off home.

CAN'T DECIDE WHETHER TO GO UP OR DOWN

律師

A MEDIATOR CONTEMPLATES SUICIDE

Meditation is a roaring success. Clients coming to lawyers for a bit of a dust up confusingly find everyone being sickeningly nice to each other. Mediation provides the relief that the fight is over and the knowledge that your opponents didn't get everything they wanted either.

Why didn't we lawyers think of this before? Well in legal terms, it wasn't so long ago when there was trial by battle where the parties slogged it out—bloody, but fun to watch. So lawyers have moved on.

9. Rough justice in clubs

Club membership has so much more to offer than a game of tennis, bowls or a few social drinks. Add to that intrigue, gossip, conflict, the cut and thrust of the committee meeting which spills over to the AGM and it can be all out war.

You may not know the club rules back to front, however, every committee member and any member being disciplined should know the Law of Natural Justice which has two basic rules-

Rule 1   No bias. Even the most hardnosed committee should be using words like 'we want to listen to your side', 'we want to be fair to you', 'have you anything else to say?' before finding an accused member guilty as charged. Punching the air and other expressions of joy at an exclusion or suspension is behaviour that committee members should try to avoid.

Rule 2   Every person is entitled to a fair hearing. This means that the accused member is to be given reasonable notice of the hearing and written details of the allegations in advance.

These two rules contain a multitude of challenges for committee decision-makers. Courts are not concerned about the decisions that committees make but courts deal with challenges to the procedures committees use to reach those decisions. Even if a member has broken club rules, a failure by the committee to adopt the correct disciplinary procedures can make committee actions unlawful. If a breach of natural justice has occurred, the court can set aside the committee's ruling.

律師

GREAT LAW SCHOOLS OF THE DEEP

There will be committee members out there for whom this pussy-footing around is just too hard. The Hanging Judge Jeffries approach is certainly quick. But if it does go before the court, judges will expect justice in the clubs not only to be done, but to be seen to be done.

10. Don't speak to strangers

Who has not imagined themselves rushing to the front of a plane or a theatre when the shout goes up, 'Is there a doctor in the house?'

In lawyer dreams it is, 'Is there a lawyer in the house?' but they would quickly need to advise themselves that giving advice to strangers is a good way to get themselves sued, whereas it is quite safe, although utterly spineless, to keep in the background and maybe hand out a few business cards. This is not only the case with lawyers and doctors but also plumbers, electricians and maybe piano tuners. If fact anyone who provides a service to the public.

Why is this? Well, it's because of the law of negligence. Everybody knows what this is. Who hasn't leant out of their car window and shouted to a fellow motorist, 'You're being negligent' or words to that effect. Negligence does not need malice. The motorist going the wrong way down the one way street, intentionally or not, still gathers abuse. Generally, doctors do not deliberately kill their patients (although they may experience a great temptation in some cases).

Where you have a written contract for the service you provide you can set out the terms and try to limit your liability. You can at least describe the advice you have given so there is no misunderstanding. But giving advice to strangers has no such protection.

When a person is injured or their property is damaged they look around for someone who can pay, such as a business or a Council. For obvious reasons there is no point in suing someone who has got neither the resources nor the backing of an insurance company, because even if you win you won't receive any money.

You can't get blood out of a stone—but many try.

THE JUDGE FOUND HIMSELF DROPPING OFF AGAIN. THESE ALL NIGHT POKER GAMES HAD TO STOP

PART 4

Intellectual Property

Although the Financial Times reports that *Intellectual Property is today's competitive weapon ...one of the key drivers of business competitiveness in the 21st century* many business owners are a little hazy on what their intellectual property rights are exactly.

There are five areas of Intellectual Property law-

• copyright

• trade marks

• designs

• patents and

• trade secrets.

Intellectual Property is the product of your mind. It can be far more valuable than any real property, for instance the Coca Cola formula. You can create value in your own business by protecting your unique ideas using Intellectual Property law. Once your ideas are packaged the right way they can be sold, and sold and sold.

1.   Copyright—are you sure it's yours?

If you are a twisted individual who likes to steer conversations towards subjects where only you have researched the answers, then copyright is your chance to shine.

Copyright protects your creative works such as anything you write down, music you compose, those cute photos of the dog—all sorts of creative stuff.

If you produce quality writing, artwork or, say, training materials which are desirable, financial or otherwise, then some enterprising person may copy your work. Copying original work is a copyright infringement. The easiest way to deal with this is violently, however, this is illegal, even if it is cheaper than using the law. A copyright lawyer can spend lots of your money shoring up your case unless you have taken certain precautions.

The best way of advising you how to protect your work is by telling you the common defences that you can expect from infringers who are copying your copyright work-

THEN HE SAID THAT IS VERY REASONABLE, THANK YOU

PSYCH

律師

PROPERTY LAWYER POST-FEE STRESS DISORDER

*   *You gave me permission.*
    This can be implied.
    Therefore you should
    be careful when allowing
    others to use your
    work. For instance,
    allowing others to copy

information from your website should have some terms and conditions attached.

- *You copied me,* or more simply, *Prove you own it.* Proving it can be costly and surprisingly difficult. When your lawyer suggests that you call your mother as a witness you know that you are in desperate straits.

- *I didn't know it was copied.* However, copyright infringement does not need intention—the act is enough.

Here are four things you can do to protect your work-

1. Keep your rough drafts— they are good evidence that you created the original.

2. Put the work in an envelope and post it to your lawyer or someone else who would be believed by the court to establish it was in existence on a certain day. Or use some other means to record that date.

3. Use written agreements called licences when letting other people use your copyright work.

4. Use the copyright symbol—©—your name and year. You don't need to register copyright, and there is no charge to use the symbol, just type it on the document. This warns people that they are dealing with your copyright work. Get written assignments of any copyright work which you buy from someone else.

The test for originality is quite low so you can get close to borrowing other peoples ideas and still come out with copyright works that are all yours.

Here are six more things to know about copyright-

M Mini franchise-you can create a work once and then licence numerous people to use your copyright work. This is what Microsoft and the software industry do.

A Automatic. No registration or form of words is required—it is protected as soon as you produce it.

L Life. Generally, copyright lasts for the life of the author plus seventy years.

I International. The powerful record, film and software lobbies have been successfully working with governments for years to have similar laws in each country to enhance copyright protection.

C Cheap. Creating a copyright work costs nothing. No registration fees, no legal documents.

E Expensive. Resolving even the most basic copyright issue can be extremely expensive so try to document your rights where you are dealing with copyright work which is important to you now or may be in the future.

Now you are aware of copyright, paranoia may set in. Please be assured that not everybody is infringing your copyright although it is easily done by down- loading or photocopying, but not by looking at you in a funny way.

A copyright infringement win can be very satisfying. Not only does it sound great but it gives the impression that there is something worth taking. However, don't expect a financial killing unless you have really suffered tangible loss. I don't mean hurt feelings.

With the right advice, copyright actions can be settled immediately on the basis of a written undertaking not to do it again, sometimes a small payment and both parties move on. With the wrong advice you can spook the other side and it can result in expensive emergency court proceedings.

Finally, you will be relieved to hear that the quality of your creative work is not put under the microscope. In the law of copyright the courts protect your work however lousy it is. If as a writer, artist or other creative sort of person your work stinks, then the good news is that you do not have a copyright problem. Copyright infringers are just too busy I'm afraid.

2. Use or lose your trade marks

At some stage as a business owner you may achieve enough success to register your business name and/or products as a trade mark.

Just like joining the Free Masons or Opus Dei there are certain things which are not widely known by outsiders (the Great Unmarked), such as-

1. When you register a trade mark you must choose a class of goods or services to which the trade mark applies. You only get protection for that limited class. Getting the class right is tricky. A trade mark can be owned by several different people for different products provided it does not cause confusion. For instance, you would not get away with using Coca Cola for, say, shoes.

2. Use it or lose it. If you do not continue to use your mark for one of the purposes stated in your registered class then you could lose the protection.

3. Use by others of your trade mark, not in the course of trade or business, is not a trade mark infringement.

4. Others can use your trade mark to identify your products. Even if it is to say how much better their products are, however, they had better be right.

5. You can use your own name. So Scotland's MacDonalds clan are quite safe. So too, are Mr and Mrs Microsoft, if they are still out there.

6. Trade marks generally apply to one country but the principles are similar internationally. In any country where you have not registered your trade mark it can be owned by others.

7. Stamping ® meaning *registered* and **TM** meaning *applied for* all over your products is fun, but not essential for protection. However, it may greatly assist any court action.

As a new trade mark owner, reminding other business owners that you have a mark and they don't, is pathetic and childish, but hard to resist.

律師

HIS WIFE HAD ADVISED HIM
NOT TO HAVE THE CLIENT SURVEY

3. Defending your name

When starting your business not only did you devise a brilliant business name but your mum liked it too. Now you have a registered company name or business name and an internet domain name, all usually established on a first come first served basis.

None of these registrations mean that you own the name. But as long as you maintain your business as an unsuccessful entity, which most small businesses owners seem to manage, probably no one is going to bother you. But if you achieve success expect look-alike companies and domain names or complete rip-offs to surface, all selling similar products to your own.

The most straightforward method of protecting your business name and products is a registered trade mark. The drawback is that registration costs money, so most small businesses wait until a threat arises before sneaking out to apply for a trade mark, hoping for the best. This can work.

律師

THE MAGISTRATE STARTED TO SUSPECT SOME COLLUSION BETWEEN DEFENCE AND PROSECUTION

Trying to stop someone using your unregistered trade mark is a legal pain in the neck, but it can be done. Usually you must show-

* Sales figures and all sorts of other evidence to indicate your reputation.

- Some deception or misleading conduct by others, for example, passing off their products as yours. Evidence of confusion is good.

- Damage to your business, like lost sales or customer complaints, leading to loss of reputation.

With a registered trade mark you do not need to prove goodwill or reputation and therefore it is relatively easy to prosecute offenders or to prove your case in a civil court.

Increasingly, businesses are attaching more importance to their brand and therefore their business name. Businesses need to ensure that their name is protected and exercise caution by not inadvertently using trade marks belonging to another company or trade marks that are deceptively similar.

4. Safeguarding designs in a material world

You are a supplier of cups, cutlery or curtains. Your customers constantly want different designs. Do you independently come up with each idea yourself? Or do you look at what others have done and use their designs with or without a few changes?

Everyone knows what a design is until you produce one and you want to protect it using the law. Then you are faced with other intellectual property rights such as copyright and patents. It can become confusing. For design think Italian, fashion, camp, shapes and patterns. For patents think nutty professor. For artistic copyright think Rembrandt. Copyright, in general does not protect designs for some industrial type mass-produced purpose.

The Law is an Ass – make sure it doesn't bite yours!

Almost every country has design laws and they differ in registration procedure and whether or not an unregistered design has protection. It is best to protect a design by registration.

To illustrate what you can expect in design law here are five points to know about design in Australia where I now practise-

1. Registering a design gives you a monopoly for ten years.

2. You can register a design cheaply and easily. But if you want to enforce it you must pay extra to have it examined.

3. You can challenge another's registered design by insisting that it be examined. If you are successful the other's registration will be revoked.

4. To register your design it must be new and distinctive, not substantially similar in overall impression to the design of another in this country or overseas. Court cases can have a 'yes it is', 'no it isn't' feel to them.

5. Spare parts are not protected by design law in order to promote competition in that market, for example, vehicle spare parts. You can infringe another's design right by making, importing, selling or hiring products using their design

There is a registered and unregistered design right system in Europe. In the UK unregistered designs can be protected for fifteen years and registered designs for twenty-five years.

Most people don't see very much wrong in copying a design—unless it is their own design being copied and then they can get very upset.

5. Death, where is thy swing?

You live to play golf but even after years of playing, your game is still lousy. Your spouse thinks that you are the problem (no change there) but you are convinced that it is your golf equipment. After a few drinks at the clubhouse, you have a brilliant idea for an invention.

You are not alone. The fairway to the local patent office is becoming very crowded. There are over 1,000 patents dealing with tee shapes and golf ball dimples alone.

A patent gives you a monopoly over a product, usually for twenty years.

Here are some things to know-

The Law is an Ass – make sure it doesn't bite yours!

1. Speak to a patent agent before publishing or using the product, otherwise you may lose the right to patent it. If you must tell someone then use a confidentiality agreement. Even if it is your mother. In some countries like Australia, there is a twelve-month grace period.

2. A patent covers one country. Patent rules around the world are similar but not the same. There is an international registration process.

3. Unless you are a genius then someone may have had a similar idea before you. There are many databases, some worldwide, where a check can be made of 'Prior Art', that is, other people's patents. This can save you a lot of money and wasted dreams.

4. Usually, a provisional application is made to secure the date followed by a full application within twelve months. Publication takes place after eighteen months.

5. People think twice before infringing a patent. But if the patent is valuable, infringers are likely to defend on the basis that your patent is invalid, for example, it is obvious or not new.

律師

HOW'S THE CASE GOING THEN?

Patents are no longer the preserve of nutty professors—even some business methods can be registered. Of course, patent court proceedings are horrendously expensive (but you guessed that didn't you?)

6. Confidentiality—protecting trade secrets

If you are a paranoid uncommunicative boss who can't delegate you may not have much of a business and your employees probably don't like you, but you get full marks in the confidentiality stakes.

Despite the proliferation of electronic listening devices, which could make spying on your competitors so much more fun, it is more likely that your confidential business information will be taken by your employees.

To protect themselves employers can put a confidentiality clause in employment agreements. Those employers who have not quite got round to confidentiality clauses will be relieved to know that the Law of Confidentiality imposes on employees an unwritten implied duty to keep things secret. Not only whilst employed but after leaving employment. One of the most cost effective methods of protection is to ensure that your employees know of this implied duty.

But what is confidential information? There are generally three things a court will consider—

1. Was there a quality of confidentiality about the information? For instance, was it an essential part of the goodwill of the business, a client list or the Coca Cola formula?

2. Was the information given in circumstances which suggest that it was confidential? The practice of stamping documents 'confidential' is good evidence. But it can often be taken up with relish by the whole staff stamping everything 'confidential' which somewhat devalues this protection. So too, strong procedures for secure storage and handling of confidential information can be undermined by a culture of non-compliance.

律師

WELL I'LL BE! ANOTHER AUSTRALIAN SOLICITOR

3. Was the information used to the detriment of the giver? For instance, are your former employees selling the same goods? Or has the information been passed to a competitor?

Not everything labelled confidential will be treated as such by the courts. Judges need to see some real loss, not just hurt pride.

Businesses nowadays, big and small, have been revolutionised by the internet and computers. There are certain things you should know about e-law. If your new computer system brings your business to its knees then you must know what to do. This is one contract that a lawyer should look at and negotiate as it is crucial to you and too often new computer systems do go wrong.

PART 5

e-law made easy

Your employees can get you into a lot of trouble using office email and your marketing efforts could attract spam penalties.

If you use your website to trade internationally then you should have some idea of the rules.

1. Avoid a contract minefield

When upgrading or renewing your business computer system you will probably purchase software, hardware and services too. The supplier will give you a draft contract. You read it and give it to a lawyer who specialises in reviewing software contracts. Only kidding—you hate lawyers. You sign the contract and put your copy in a drawer.

There are a number of potential problems with this course of action. Here are just four—

- **The exclusion clause**
  This limits the liability of the supplier. For instance, your claim is limited to the equivalent of the price that you paid for the software and then the software and services offered by the supplier are so ineffective your business is brought to its knees.

- **Who is going to use the software?**
  Make sure it is the name of the right company or employee and that the type of licence is appropriate for the requirements of your business. (There are about twelve types of licence.) Any changes in the licence use will cost you money, for example, you get the name wrong or you open a branch office or want to sell your business and transfer the software.

- **Escrow agreement**
  The source code of the software should be held by a third party in case the supplier goes bust or just loses interest. Otherwise, you will not be able to make changes to the software as your business grows or your requirements change.

- **Termination**
  The contract will contain provisions dealing with what happens on termination of the contract or if the matter is going badly wrong. For instance, the contract may provide that if you do not hand over the money when due you can't use the computer system. It may force you to hand over the money before you are satisfied with the computer system.

Are the software suppliers sometimes quick to charge high fees for permission to use the software in ways not provided for in the contract? Well yes. In the software business this is called 'stiffing' and happens too often.

Computer contracts need to be carefully negotiated. Be warned.

2. Cyberspace and the law of the net

'Startrek' highlighted the potential dangers of cyberspace.

Your website attracts customers but making the deal is usually done by telephone and/or email. However, the opportunity for e-commerce in terms of volume and speed of transactions is launching small business owners into cyberspace.

Thankfully, lawyers have been in cyberspace (some would say for centuries) doing a bit of path finding. At first, panic led to complex laws which seemed both urgent and essential but were not, for example, electronic signatures. Then things calmed down.

Five tips for internet trading—

1. You are in one country and your customer is in another. Which country's laws apply? If it is not specified in your terms and conditions (or you haven't got any) then who knows? However, should your customer be a consumer, expect his choice of law to prevail as most countries have laws that favour consumers.

2. Your exclusions, limitations and other methods of dodging liability are unlikely to work if you do not choose which law applies.

3. A 'link' referring the customer to your terms of business is sufficient.

4. When do you spring your terms and conditions on your customer-—before or after you make the deal? After would be fun, but usually, international law says you inform the customer of the terms and conditions before the customer hits the 'accept' button. Otherwise, they do not apply.

NOW LET'S HEAR THE ARGUMENT FOR THE ROAST BEEF

律師

MRS JUSTICE SMITH WAITED FOR HER HUSBAND TO DECIDE WHAT HE WANTED FOR DINNER

5. But when is the deal concluded? As with a purchase in a shop, you offer to buy and the shop, at the till, decides if it is going to sell. Shops that underprice items get a chance to correct their mistake at the till. But on a website, with automatic confirmation, the technology sticks you with even the most ludicrous contract, quickly, efficiently and as many times as required.

In summary, lawyers have deployed in cyberspace a legal framework which is as dull as dishwater and very similar to what has gone before. 'Oh joy' I hear you say.

3.   The revealing truth of email

If you are an employer who only hires staff who use office email sensibly then what can I say but 'Yeah, right'.

Just as the art of correspondence was being phased out by the telephone along came email and now everybody is emailing from teenagers to terrorists. This is a rum turn of events for lawyers. There was skill in questioning witnesses to glean the truth and lots of room for ambiguity. Now email reveals all.

Employers are liable for the actions of employees who are innovative and enthusiastic office email users.

律師

MRS B. COULD TELL WHEN HER HUSBAND WAS IN THE MOOD FOR AN ARGUMENT

There are three main risks—

1. Why do employees send emails containing blue humour to prudish tetchy employees who are covered by the sexual harassment laws and were planning to leave anyway? I don't know, but on the positive side, it gives the harassed employee an opportunity to complain or leave and claim constructive dismissal.

2. Some employees think that no legal contract can be made by email. They are wrong.

3. If your employee decides to insult someone using your email you can be liable, especially if it is defamatory. Instruct employees intending to make defamatory comments by email to use the telephone instead, or even better, shout out the window, as it is harder to prove.

If you are a big company or a small business finding it hard to do sales calls then draft an email policy in consultation with everyone. If you are a small business owner do what you always do. Let it go until there is a problem and then respond with a knee-jerk reaction when something goes wrong.

No legal proceedings are complete without the smoking gun email that blows a legal case out of the water. As Clint Eastwood said in Dirty Harry, 'Make my day'.

4.   Stand by your spam

Spammers are evil people who deserve to be punished. But what if you are the spammer? Spamming is as easy as sending a few unsolicited selling emails or just trying to promote your product too hard using email.

Hopefully, you can resist this, but can your sales staff? Your brilliant weekly motivational sessions have turned a bunch of no-hopers into a ruthless selling machine. The only thing stopping them is your lousy product. In desperation they turn to the dark side—spam. If reported as the business owner you are likely to face a heavy financial penalty.

Try these ten rules to avoid a spam penalty—

1.   DO have a policy and let your staff know what it is. This can be as easy as your staff reading these words. However, the judge would probably prefer more.

2.   DO NOT send 'selling' spam by email, fax or text without having the addressee's consent.

3.   You CAN SEND informative unsolicited information but do not sell (even a little bit) in the electronic communication.

4.   DO say clearly who you are.

5.   DON'T use mailing data carelessly.

6.   DO NOT use a harvested address list. (This is one created by software collecting emails from the Internet.)

7. DO apologise quickly to prevent being reported. One telephone call can save you a lot of hassle and money.

DARWIN'S THEORY OF BARRISTERS

律師

8. You CAN SEND spam to publicised email addresses where the person is in business and clearly does not mind receiving such emails.

9. DO have an unsubscribe facility in the email.

10. DO deal with unsubscribe requests within five days.

If your abject apology fails then your policy may save you.

If not, on a positive note, your prosecution may be what your competitor's sales team need to stop them from trying it on.

5. The internet and pornography

Child pornography is sick and a serious crime. Other pornography may be considered bad by some but it is often legal. The distinction is important for all employers.

Some of your employees might download pornography from the internet. Why? Maybe they don't have broadband at home. Or perhaps they live with their mum. In any event, it is a growing problem.

Pornography can lead to witch-hunts and mistakes can be made. Like the angry mob in the UK, railing against paedophiles, that attacked a paediatrician by mistake.

An immediate sacking of a porn-downloading employee not only makes you feel good but leaves everyone feeling that little bit sanctimonious. The downside is that, as the boss, you will carry the can if you have got it wrong. Accusing someone of downloading pornography can be in the serious defamation camp if you are wrong or cannot prove it.

YOUR HONOUR, I DON'T HAVE A LONG SUBMISSION TO MAKE

律師

GREAT MOMENTS IN EVOLUTION

Sacking a person downloading porn can get rid of a difficult employee. But the next time it could be your star performer. What do you do then? What if several of your employees are caught at once?

On the other hand, child pornography in the workplace is a police matter. Computer evidence requires careful treatment and is easy to contaminate. Isolate the computer and tell the police. With child pornography the offence is having it on your machine. So it is easy to put yourself in the frame if you procrastinate and don't remove or report the images quickly. A computer's delete button does not really delete data—it just hides it ready to be revealed by the police forensic expert. This can be a two-edged sword for you.

Internet pornography in the workplace is trouble. Your knee jerk reaction can make the situation worse.

And to sum up ...

It has been a lot easier to sum up thirty odd years experience than I thought it would be. I am relieved that I have managed to fill up more that the back of a postage stamp. I am not sorry that I have left out the rubbish dump of legal information which now is only a few clicks away from any legal practitioner.

I hope you find this book one that you can refer to often; one which you can go back to again and again as you encounter legal issues. And perhaps a number of readers may feel enthused enough to delve further into some of the legal subjects covered.

However, I am aware, as Richard Ingrams said, 'When lawyers talk about the law, normal human beings begin to think about something else'.

Further Information

If you want to know more, go to www.brennanlaw.com.au

There you'll find CD products expanding on each legal area covered in the book and free information as well.

PAUL BRENNAN

Paul Brennan was born in London. He has worked in the law in various countries including the UK, Canada, Hong Kong and Australia.

He has drawn legal cartoons for the Australian Financial Review, the Hong Kong Tatler and other publications from time to time.

In creating the *101 Reasons To Kill All the Lawyers* blog he explained, "I decided on 101 reasons as I didn't want to depress the entire legal profession by having 1,001."

He is in practice with his wife Diane on Queensland's Sunshine Coast. They have four children.

Other books by the author go to:

http://www.amazon.com/Paul-Brennan/e/B001KMQFEC

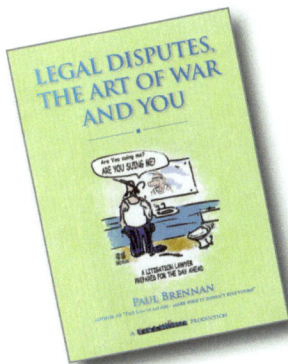

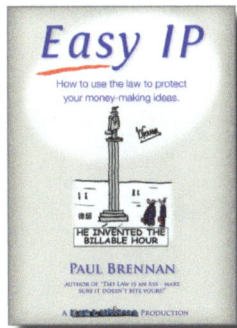

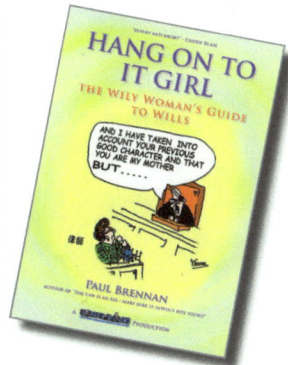

CONTACT US ON
(07) 5438 8199 or
email: info@lawanddisorder.com.au

BRENNANS
SOLICITORS

B

律師

SPONSORED by
www.brennanlaw.com.au